Chronicles of Nevermore and Forevermore

Kathy Stubblefield

Archway Publishing books may be ordered through booksellers or by contacting:

Archway Publishing
1663 Liberty Drive
Bloomington, IN 47403
www.archwaypublishing.com
1 (888) 242-5904

ISBN: 978-1-4808-8079-5 (sc)
ISBN: 978-1-4808-8078-8 (e)

Print information available on the last page.

Archway Publishing rev. date: 8/6/2019

I opened the door to the feed barn and stepped inside, hoping to find some hay for my chicken nest boxes. As my eyes adjusted to the dim light, I noticed two eggs in the corner on the old wood floor. They were speckled, as if someone had splattered them with brown paint. I thought, *No, that couldn't have happened.*

I picked them up for closer inspection. They were bigger than chicken eggs and smaller than goose eggs, with brown speckles all over. I knew they would never have a chance, even if the mother bird came back, because a family of egg-loving racoons had also made the old barn their home. I thought taking them home and incubating them would give the young ones a chance. I already had an incubator set up to hatch chicken eggs.

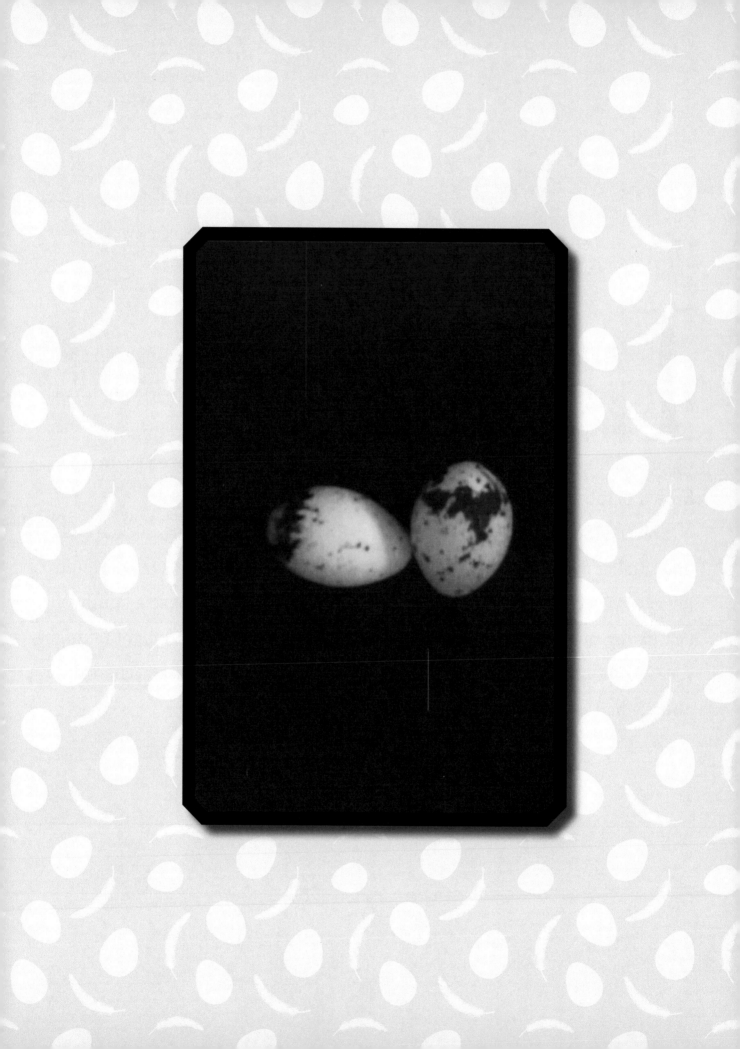

I thought they might be wild turkeys or even some type of a duck. A little more research indicated that they might be vulture eggs. *Oh great!* I thought. *What have I gotten myself into?*

My curiosity took over, and I put the eggs into the incubator on March 9, 2013, doubting the possibility of them ever hatching. I put an X on one side of the eggs and an O on the other side and turned them two to three times daily. I also adjusted the humidity and temperature as I would for chicken eggs.

After five days, I candled the eggs by using a bright light to check their growth. Nothing was visible yet. With brown speckles all over the shell, it was hard to see developing embryos.

After a couple of weeks, I candled them again. It looked as if something was developing, but it was hard to tell.

After a month, still no hatch. I was disappointed but kept turning them and waited a little longer, just in case.

Then on Saturday night, April 13, I was in the room with the incubator, and I could hear a huffing sound—like someone was breathing hard. Looking inside, I could see a hairline crack on each egg. What was going to hatch? What was making that weird sound: a dinosaur? a turtle? a snake?

I hardly slept at all that night in anticipation of the hatch. Jumping out of bed at 5:30 a.m., I was just in time to see one of the creatures emerge from its shell. It had a black beak and light-brown fur all over, like a teddy bear. Fur? Yes, fur. Or down. It wasn't feathers. Nor was it naked like other baby birds.

The other bird hatched about 8:30 Sunday morning, April 14, 2013. Who would have known the identical little fur balls could be so cute! It was love at first sight.

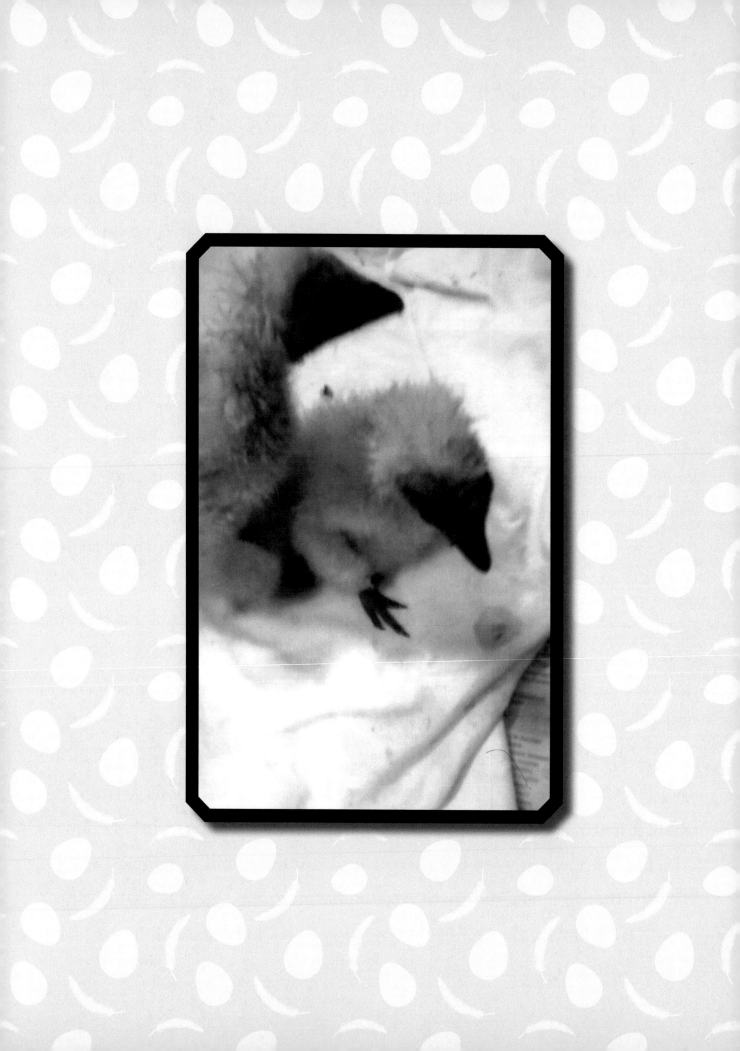

I made a commitment at that point to raise them and release them into the wild, just like Tweety, the baby mockingbird I had rescued from the cat. Tweety grew and was eager to get out of the cage and make a life of his own.

The next hurdle was feeding them. According to internet sources, baby birds need a high-protein diet. The mother birds feed the babies by regurgitation, and I felt a medicine dropper would work. With enough milk to thin the gruel, raw eggs and canned cat food became their first meal, which they eagerly gobbled up. When they heard my voice, they knew food was on the way, so they fluttered and flapped their furry wings and hopped around, huffing and puffing. Huffin and Puffin seemed like good names at the time.

Never having seen a vulture up close, I found it awesome how perfectly and wonderfully equipped God made them. The end of the top beak curved down into a "tooth" or maybe better described as a "hook." This feature gave the species tremendous leverage and grip and, as I soon learned, was very sharp. Literal hand-feeding might result in the loss of a finger, as instinctively they nuzzled between my fingers while trying to feed. Both of them were hungry at once, and feeding with a medicine dropper three or four times a day became difficult. A plastic spoon solved the problem since they could both eat at once. They quickly adapted to the new situation, and my fingers were spared in the process. I hoped they would live and thrive, and thrive they did.

The April nights were cool, so I kept them inside in a cage. After about a month, I moved them outside to a bigger cage during the day and into the chicken pen at night. Weighing about a pound each, there were still no characteristic black feathers—just teddy bear fur or down all over.

Without feathers, they couldn't fly. I turned them out of the pen during the day to mingle with the chickens. The chickens ignored them unless they were trying to eat their food. At night, they roosted with the chickens. Since they couldn't fly yet, they walked and hopped around, following me everywhere. The hand-feeding must have made them gentle and domesticated. Sitting at my feet outside, they could be petted and picked up.

Gradually, at about two months old, black feathers appeared. Most of the fur grew out, and the birds began to fly a little. Sometimes they flew up to my arm and even to the top of my head, especially if I had on my straw hat. It was comical to see their awkward landings, sometimes tumbling and slamming into whatever was in the way. By the middle of July, they perched on the fence posts and began roosting in trees at night.

Fully feathered by August, daily flights, especially in the evenings, became a ritual. Meals consisted of whatever we were having, usually with a lot of meat. They did not relish vegetables and fruits.

In the mornings, they waited for breakfast at the front door, which was barricaded with a four-foot fence, until they figured out how to fly over it.

Because they were identical, I needed a way to tell them apart. One was more docile and would sit quietly at my feet. She became Forevermore. She sat still to have her toenails painted as well as a tiara of fingernail polish and glitter on her head feathers. The other bird was feistier. He would flutter and huff when I made him stay out of the house or car, so I named him Nevermore.

Both loved to nibble on everything, especially my shoe strings and the cuffs on my cutoffs. Most of the time they were gentle, but sometimes they gnawed a little too hard, especially when hungry. People had a hard time believing they were tame and gentle and could be petted. They would even come when called.

Both were curious and had to check out everything, especially my old garden shoe on the front porch and the rubber trim on car doors, probably because they wanted to get into the car and travel too.

Forevermore's curiosity got the best of her, and she got her beak slammed in a car door once. It must have really hurt because she walked away shaking her head. Finally, after about two hours, she felt better and was able to eat.

Their curiosity was more like being nosey. On game day, two airplanes were circling low, pulling banners. The birds flew off after them, soaring high in the sky. After a couple of hours, they returned. I don't know if they ever caught up with the planes, but apparently they gave up trying.

Domesticated and tame didn't adequately describe them. They were helpful, or maybe just plain nosey. They helped check the oil in the car, go after the mail, and do the laundry, not to mention their gardening abilities of riding along on the tiller and breaking up dirt clods. The fearless duo also hopped along when I mowed grass or hoed in the garden.

After roosting on the house for a couple of months, the birds decided to sleep on a utility pole across the street. But they arrived at the door at dawn and waited for breakfast, which was usually scrambled eggs.

It was awesome to see the birds up close, the waterproofed black feathers in perfect pattern with a fifty-inch wingspan that folded to a mere eight inches across the back. Next to their bodies was a fur lining.

I can only imagine being there when Jesus looked at the birds in the air and said that God sees whenever one falls. How much more does He care for us! I have been privileged to see the birds up close, as few people have, being perfectly created by God for their purpose in life. He can likewise supply all our needs if we can only trust Him!

The scorching, dry summer days gradually turned into the cooler days of fall. The birds' flights became longer. Eventually, they came home only during the hottest part of the day to rest under the shade trees. Then after supper, they flew to the utility pole.

The days grew shorter and the cold, icy winds of winter set in. During the cold, rainy days, the birds stayed close, roosting in the shed. Then they took more flights on milder days.

As usual, the warmer days of spring followed, with the sun warming the awakening earth. Nevermore and Forevermore were taking longer flights, sometimes coming home only for breakfast.

One day after breakfast, they soared high into the sky. The next morning, they didn't come home. Nor the next. I watched for them each day and called their names, but they never returned.

The days turned into weeks, and I accepted the fact that they were gone forever. It was a bittersweet moment as I had known that this day would come as they found their destiny and purpose in life as God had intended when He created them. On the other hand, being captivated by their uniqueness and gentleness, their absence tore at my heart. Whenever a big black bird soared high in the sky, I was reminded of them and wondered. Still, they never came home.

One beautiful spring day, I opened the front door to let in the warm sunshine. To my amazement, standing there were Nevermore and Forevermore, patiently waiting for breakfast. And by their side were two bright-eyed, black-beaked, furry bonbons, huffing and puffing! It was a beautiful sight to see. But it was unfortunately just a dream.

One thing that wasn't a dream was something I'll never forget. The end of February brings a few days of seventy-degree weather, alternating with days of subfreezing temperatures, a sure sign that spring is on the way. March brought more bird visitors. While Nevermore and Forevermore sat quickly eating their scrambled eggs, before the chickens could get them, visitors perched on the rooftop and sat up straight, trying to look dignified. And then the air show began.

The birds flew in circles, swooping and diving, putting the Blue Angels to shame. My guess was that my birds were girls and the visitors were boys showing off, trying to impress them. All the while, they were being ignored by Nevermore and Forevermore, who, after finishing their breakfast, helped me start the lawnmower.

Who would know out of big, speckled eggs little furry bonbons

would emerge with black beaks and three little toes?

They fluttered and flapped their furry little wings when they

heard my voice, knowing their food I would bring.

They grew and grew, so gentle and sweet. I called them by name, and

they followed me everywhere I went—and had a look of love. I know.

Who would know that whenever love and care you

send, they will fly back into your life again?

Quoth the Raven, Forevermore!

Printed in the United States
By Bookmasters